PARANORMAL SEEKERS™

TRACKING BIGFOOT

JENNA VALE AND
GREG COX

rosen publishing's rosen central
New York

Published in 2019 by The Rosen Publishing Group, Inc.
29 East 21st Street, New York, NY 10010

First Edition

Library of Congress Cataloging-in-Publication Data

Names: Vale, Jenna, author. | Cox, Greg, author.
Title: Tracking Bigfoot / Jenna Vale and Greg Cox.
Description: New York : Rosen Publishing, 2019. | Series: Paranormal seekers | Includes bibliographical references and index. | Audience: Grades 5–8.
Identifiers: LCCN 2018012907| ISBN 9781508185659 (library bound) | ISBN 9781508185642 (pbk.)
Subjects: LCSH: Sasquatch—Juvenile literature.
Classification: LCC QL89.2.S2 K45 2018 | DDC 001.944—dc23
LC record available at https://lccn.loc.gov/2018012907

Manufactured in the United States of America

CONTENTS

INTRODUCTION

The Pacific Northwest of the United States is thick with forests and, for some people, mystery. Hikers leave the dense, evergreen woodlands with stories of seeing a large, apelike creature, more than 7 feet (2.13 meters) tall. Their glimpses are fleeting, supported perhaps by videos taken from a distance or photos of strange, incredibly large footprints. They say the creature has dark hair all over its body and emits a powerful stench. It moves not like a bear or a gorilla but almost like a man.

These sightings happen in places like Six Rivers National Forest, located in the northwestern area of California. Perhaps the most famous film recording of a possible Bigfoot creature was taken in Six Rivers, the Patterson-Gimlin film of 1967. Six Rivers is also located near the town of Willow Creek, which is widely known as the Bigfoot capital of the world. The town has a Bigfoot museum and can be reached by California State Route 96, which is referred to as the "Bigfoot Scenic Byway."

Interest in Bigfoot has become so pervasive that there are reported sightings even beyond the Pacific Northwest. Many people want to know if Bigfoot is real, and if so, what it actually is. An undiscovered kind of primate? A missing link in the chain of evolution from primates to humans? Members of one group known as the Sasquatch Genome Project posited in 2013 that there is an abundance of DNA evidence that supports their

Six Rivers National Forest has more than 950,000 acres (384,451 hectares) of land, with elevations ranging from sea level to nearly 7,000 feet (2,134 m). If Bigfoot is there, it'd be difficult to pinpoint!

theory that Bigfoot is some kind of human hybrid, though their claims have been controversial.

History is full of eyewitness accounts that cannot be corroborated, or confirmed, by another source. There is grainy super-8 film footage from decades ago, as well as more recent shaky videos and plaster casts of footprints that must have come from something. Because Bigfoot has become a myth as large as the ape-man's alleged size, many people think those who claim to see Bigfoot are part of a hoax or are just trying to get attention.

People want to believe, and unfortunately there are some who may seek to exploit that. Still others seem sincere in their search for Bigfoot. And all the while, popular culture continues to entertain the idea of the hairy ape-man in all manner of media.

Still, considering how far science and technology have come, one question prevails: if Bigfoot were real, wouldn't it have been found by now?

CHAPTER ONE

BIGFOOT'S BIOLOGY

What are the common elements of reported Bigfoot sightings? The creature is usually described as a large, heavy anthropoid between 7 and 10 feet (2 to 3 m) tall. With very little neck, broad shoulders, and a wide, bulky torso, an adult Bigfoot may weigh as much as 800 or 900 pounds (363 to 408 kilograms), judging from the depths to which the mysterious footprints sink. A Bigfoot's body is almost completely carpeted with thick hair or fur that is usually black or reddish brown, though there's little to no hair on its face, hands, or feet. Bigfoot doesn't wear clothes or have any tools or other artifacts, aside from simple stones it might hurl at intruders. Beyond these common elements, what more has been reported?

PAINTING A PICTURE

According to witnesses, Bigfoot has a wide and varied diet, including wild berries, nuts, roots, pine needles, and the occasional rodent or rabbit. It is also thought to dig for clams, strip the leaves from willow bushes, and wade into cold mountain streams in search of

This artist's rendering of Bigfoot displays features people commonly attribute to it: a powerful build, apelike face and head, and covered in dark hair.

salmon. In addition, Bigfoot has sometimes been accused of stealing fish, chickens, and fresh fruit from campsites as well as from isolated farms and residences. Some experts believe that Bigfoot is also capable of snaring wild deer and elk with its bare hands, but the evidence for this is sketchier. Based on these theories and reports, it would seem that Bigfoot is an omnivore, meaning that the creature subsists on both meat and plants.

Unlike all other current primates except humans, Bigfoot is said to be bipedal, meaning that it walks erect on two legs. If true, this means that the discovery of an actual, living Bigfoot could teach us much about the evolution of the human species. At present, most scientists believe that *Homo sapiens* (modern humans) are the only bipedal hominids to walk the earth and have been ever since our prehistoric cousins, the Neanderthals, died off thirty thousand years ago. But what if they're wrong and humans still share the planet with some kind of primitive ape-man—a missing link or an evolutionary offshoot that became a dead end?

GIGANTOPITHECUS AND THE FOSSIL RECORD

The fossil record proves that all sorts of human-sized primates have walked the earth in the past, many of them even more humanlike than the great apes of today. Scientists keep digging up the remains of different types of early humans, some of them over four million years old. These are called hominids, a biological family that includes modern humans as well as all supposedly extinct human ancestors. Throughout prehistory, at least fourteen different varieties of hominid have roamed free; *Homo*

This illustration depicts an early settlement of hominids during the Quaternary period, which continues today and is commonly called the Age of Humans.

sapiens has only had the world to itself for the past thirty thousand years, or so it is widely believed.

Some experts believe that Bigfoot already exists in the fossil record. A prime candidate is *Gigantopithecus blacki*, an ancient primate whose jawbones and teeth have been found in China, Vietnam, and India. This creature had two close relatives found mostly in India, *Gigantopithecus bilaspurensis* and *Gigantopithecus giganteus*.

As its name suggests, *Gigantopithecus* was as tall as—or even taller than—Bigfoot is said to be and fits the standard description of a Sasquatch very closely. This towering creature, the largest primate ever to dwell on earth, may have been as much as 10 feet (3 m) tall and 1,200 pounds (540 kg). Females were considerably smaller. *Gigantopithecus* is believed by some authorities to have walked erect on two legs, just like Bigfoot does. "Giganto" lived as recently as five hundred thousand years ago and survived into the Pliocene ice age, when a land bridge connected Siberia to Alaska. It is possible that the creature emigrated from Asia to North America, where perhaps its descendants still live today.

If nothing else, the scientifically indisputable fact that *Gigantopithecus* once existed alongside humanity's own primitive ancestors proves that a creature like Bigfoot is at least biologically possible. It should be noted, however, that *Gigantopithecus* fossils have never been found in the Americas. Because no *Gigantopithecus* leg or pelvis bones or fossils have been discovered anywhere, there is no evidence to suggest that "Giganto" was bipedal. Indeed, some scientists believe that the

BEING AN EXPERT ON BIGFOOT

When reading accounts of Bigfoot sightings and other supposed evidence, the opinions and conclusions of "experts" are often cited to support the argument for or against the creature's existence. But who are these experts, and what are their qualifications?

Grover Krantz (1931–2002) was the preeminent Bigfoot researcher. He was a professor of physical anthropology at Washington State University and an expert in evolutionary anthropology and primatology (the study of primates). At first a Bigfoot skeptic, Krantz believed the Patterson-Gimlin footage of a large, hairy ape-man was a hoax. Yet upon studying the plaster casts made from tracks gathered in Bossburg, Washington, that seem to indicate a club-footed Bigfoot, Krantz became a believer and even came to accept the authenticity of the Patterson-Gimlin film. He was a champion of the theory that Bigfoot was descended from the Asian ape *Gigantopithecus*, which at some point crossed the land bridge across the Bering Strait into North America. Once converted to belief in Bigfoot, most of Krantz's academic work was devoted to Sasquatch research, which earned him the scorn of his peers, impeded his professional advancement, and restricted funding sources for his investigations. Most of his publications and articles on the subject were ignored or mocked by the academic world.

(continued on the next page)

(continued from the previous page)

Another leading Bigfoot expert is cryptozoologist Loren Coleman. Cryptozoology is the study of animals that are legendary or whose existence has not yet been proved with biological evidence. Cryptozoology is not a recognized branch of zoology, and many people dismiss it as a pseudoscience, especially since it relies so heavily on unverified sightings, stories, and eyewitness accounts—rather than hard scientific data—for evidence. Coleman did study both anthropology and zoology and taught at several universities before retiring to devote himself to writing on cryptozoology and the related fields of animal mysteries and folklore and to the establishment of his International Cryptozoology Museum in Portland, Maine. His fieldwork and writing have centered on Native American traditions regarding Sasquatch, as well as sightings and evidence traces.

Though still often dismissed as pseudoscience or fringe science, some bright lights and highly respected authorities within the fields of zoology, primatology, and anthropology have begun to express academic interest in Bigfoot. Chimpanzee researcher and advocate Jane Goodall has expressed certainty that Bigfoot exists, and Jeffrey Meldrum, a professor of anthropology and anatomy at Idaho State University, has written academic papers evaluating Sasquatch footprints and the creature's bipedal movements.

creature's height and mass were so great that upright walking would have been nearly impossible. Most researchers believe the creature walked on all four limbs like chimpanzees and gorillas.

Many scientists also point out that *Gigantopithecus* was not a hominid, meaning it did not occupy the evolutionary branch shared by humans, chimpanzees, and bonobos, seeming to undercut the likelihood of it evolving over time into an upright, bipedal "man-ape."

BIGFOOT AND *PARANTHROPUS*

A competing theory holds that Bigfoot is some species of *Paranthropus*, part of the *Australopithecus* line of primates believed to have lived in Africa 1.2 million to 2 million years ago. *Paranthropus* had a bony ridge (called a sagittal crest) running along the top of its skull, providing extra support for its powerful jaw muscles. The Bigfoot that appears in the infamous Patterson-Gimlin film also has such a crest, giving its head a pointed appearance, and various witnesses have also described Bigfoot's head as somewhat conical.

Paranthropus was considerably smaller than "Giganto," with males only about 4 feet (1.2 m) tall and 120 pounds (54 kg). *Paranthropus* had a hairy, stocky body with long arms, a gorilla-shaped head, and gorilla-like molars for powerful chewing. It seems to have walked erect at least occasionally, like a human or a Sasquatch. Yet no *Paranthropus* fossils have ever been found outside of Africa, making the creature's theoretical

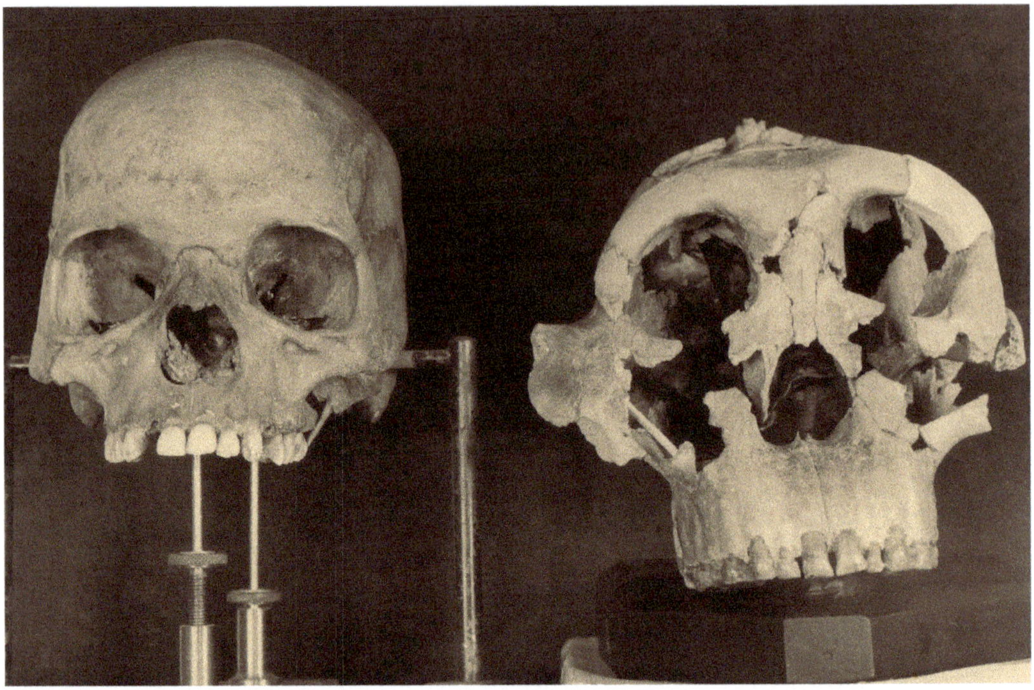

A human skull (*left*) sits beside a *Paranthropus* skull (*right*) to highlight the differences in bone structure. *Paranthropus* means "beside man."

migration to North America a problematic issue. Neither Giganto nor *Paranthropus* nor Bigfoot is known to have employed tools or fire, placing them at roughly the same level of cultural development.

A case can be made for either *Gigantopithecus* or *Paranthropus* being Bigfoot's true identity, but it is also possible that there is more than one kind of unknown hominid or hominoid roaming North America. And such a being would leave behind evidence of its existence, wouldn't it? In 2013, a man named Todd May found what he believed to be the fossilized skull of a Bigfoot creature on a trail near his home in Ogden, Utah. The area is a known hot spot for Bigfoot sightings, and May, who claimed to have multiple encounters with Bigfoot creatures throughout his life, believed he had finally found proof. May had hundreds of people weigh in on his find, and in 2016 he took the object on the road to spread the truth about Bigfoot. In a June 2016 *Times Record News* article by Claire Kowalick, however, it seemed evident that there was no need to update the fossil record just yet: "Midwestern State University Assistant Professor Jesse Carlucci, Kimball School of Geoscience, said after viewing the object is, without a doubt, just a highly weathered rock."

Todd May was searching for fossils when he came upon what he believed to be a fossilized Bigfoot skull. It weighs a whopping 70 pounds (31.8 kg) and appears to have a face.

Perhaps Bigfoot is an entirely new species unknown to science. The answer remains hidden somewhere in the wilderness, beyond humanity's present knowledge.

CHAPTER TWO

THE MYTH EMERGES

Where did the Bigfoot myth start? There are photos, videos, and plaster casts of footprints from the twentieth century, but what about before such options for recording were available? Folklore and oral tradition, or passing down stories to subsequent generations by word of mouth, have played a part in so many myths, and Bigfoot is no exception.

NATIVE AMERICAN LEGENDS

The indigenous peoples of North America have known of Bigfoot for countless generations. The myths and folklore of numerous Northwest Native American tribes are full of stories about large, smelly, hairy giants who dwell in the hills and forests, apart from humanity. These creatures go by many names—Sesquac, Seatco, Tsiatko, Dsonqua, Sokquatl, and more—but often bear a striking resemblance to the modern and popular conception of Bigfoot.

Bigfoot-like creatures can also be found on totem poles, pottery, and other Native American artifacts. Particularly intriguing are several prehistoric stone heads

Images such as this one from a 1977 film by animal tracker Ivan Marx have become common features of Bigfoot lore, but what about Bigfoot accounts that predate such documentation?

that were found along the shores of the Columbia River, between Oregon and Washington State. Although little is known about the people who carved these heads hundreds of years ago, the chiseled stones feature distinctly apelike faces, even though ancient Northwest tribes should have had no knowledge of any primate except man. With no exposure to chimps or gorillas or even monkeys, whom could these forgotten sculptors have been trying to depict except Sasquatch?

CLOSE SHAVES

The prospect of accidentally running into an inhuman creature over 7 feet (2.13 m) tall is a frightening one, but how dangerous is Bigfoot? In most modern accounts of Bigfoot encounters, the creature appears more interested in avoiding humans than in attacking them, but there are older stories in which the Sasquatch behaves much more aggressively.

A Canadian prospector named Albert Ostman repeatedly claimed to have been abducted and temporarily held hostage by an entire family of Sasquatches—a father, a mother, and two young children—back in 1924. Trapped in a remote valley near coastal British Columbia, Canada, he spent a couple of days observing the creatures, who mostly left him alone. He finally managed to escape by tricking the large male Bigfoot into trying some of the prospector's powdered tobacco. The noxious snuff made the creature so violently ill that

Ostman was able to flee the valley during the resulting confusion.

The very same year, on Mount Saint Helens in Washington State, another set of prospectors fought off a hostile band of enraged Bigfoots after the men shot (and possibly killed) a large simian creature in what is now called Ape Canyon. The prospectors' log cabin was besieged at night by gorilla-like "mountain devils" who shrieked and howled as they hurled heavy rocks at the walls and roof of the cabin. At one point during that terrifying evening, a hairy arm reached into the cabin through a hole in the wall, groping for an ax, before being repelled by gunfire. The frightened miners later described their attackers as having "the appearance of huge gorillas," their massive bodies covered all over with long black hair. They also found numerous footprints, roughly 2 feet (61 centimeters) in length.

SASQUATCH IN CAPTIVITY

In 1884, according to the *Victoria Daily Colonist*, a strange creature, "something of a gorilla type," was captured alongside a railroad near the village of Yale in British Columbia. The hairy monster, nicknamed "Jacko," was reportedly spying on a train when the passengers spotted him. The train was stopped so that a number of the crewmen could chase after the creature. They eventually knocked Jacko unconscious with a rock, tied him up with a heavy rope, then shipped him to Yale.

WHAT'S IN A NAME?

"Sasquatch" is not truly a Native American word for the giant, hairy, bipedal creature that is part of the Native American folkloric tradition. Rather, the word was coined by a Canadian newspaperman, J. W. Burns, who wrote a series of articles on the Native American tales of the giant forest-dwelling ape-man. He borrowed the Native American word *sesquac*, which means "wild man" and refers to a mythical or natural being that possesses a spirit better left alone. From this loan word, Burns created "Sasquatch."

The name "Bigfoot" was not invented until 1958, over three decades after the Ape Canyon incident. The word first appeared in the *Humboldt Times* of Eureka, California, in an article reporting on construction worker Gerald Crew's discovery of 16-inch (41 cm) humanlike footprints. The whole notion of an unknown man-monster running around the Northwest did not really become widespread until national newspapers started covering the topic in the late 1950s. Nevertheless, a 1924 Oregon newspaper account of the Mount Saint Helens prospectors' bizarre story mentions that "Indians have told of the 'mountain devils' for 60 years," and that tracks such as the miners described "have been seen by forest rangers and prospectors for years." In other words, Bigfoot was haunting the forests long before he became famous.

Jacko was watched over by a Yale resident named George Tilbury. The creature remained largely silent but occasionally emitted a sound that was described as half-growl and half-bark. He ate berries and milk while in captivity. He wasn't fed any meat, out of fear that the taste of meat would turn the beast savage. Judging from the description in the original report, Jacko sounds like he would have been a young Sasquatch, not yet fully grown. He was 4 feet 7 inches (1.4 m) tall, approximately 127 pounds (57 kg), and "resembles a human being

Mountains loom over the town of Yale in British Columbia around 1890, not long after the events surrounding the mysterious Jacko.

with one exception, his entire body, excepting his hand (or paws) and feet are covered with glossy hair about 1 inch [2.5 cm] long."

Much to the extreme frustration of Bigfoot researchers, who have spent countless hours poring through old newspapers looking for more information about this incident, no record remains of whatever happened to Jacko. There had been some talk of shipping the creature to London, England, for exhibit. Some people in the Yale area believed that Jacko was sent East by train but died in transit. Some skeptics have questioned whether the Jacko incident actually happened. If the *Victoria Daily Colonist* is to be believed, however, it remains the only documented account of a Bigfoot creature being captured alive.

MORE THAN A TEDDY BEAR

No less a personage than Theodore Roosevelt provided a secondhand account of an unusually violent Bigfoot encounter said to have occurred in a remote corner of Idaho sometime in the mid-1800s. In his book *The Wilderness Hunter*, first published in 1892, the future president told of a young fur trapper who, after being stalked for a day or two by a smelly, two-legged creature, returned to his camp one evening to find his trapping partner dead, his neck broken and mauled. In recounting the story, Roosevelt writes, "The footprints of the unknown beast-creature, printed deep in the soft soil, told the whole story."

The crewman seen operating this bulldozer would not be able to overturn such a piece of equipment—bulldozers can weigh many tons!

While modern accounts of Bigfoot encounters have been markedly more peaceful, there is still a trace of violence associated with the creature. In 1962, near the Hoopa Indian Reservation, which is not far from Willow Creek, California, there was a strange incident that many came to consider a test of a Bigfoot's strength. In Michele Bigley's 2012 book about the area entitled *Backroads & Byways of Northern California*, she writes of the incident, "After the crews had begun work on the road, they returned to the project site in the morning to find their bulldozers turned over, 500-pound [227 kg] tires thrown down the mountain, and giant footprints littering the scene. The Hoopa shrugged in the I-told-you-so manner of the knowing, and soon after, Bigfoot hunters began arriving like crazy." No other evidence of Bigfoot was found around the construction site in the days that followed, but that of course has not deterred enthusiasts from looking. Many travel the Eyesee Road on their way to the Bigfoot capital, and the search for evidence is tireless.

CHAPTER THREE

FINDINGS IN THE FOREST

Bigfoot sightings, of varying degrees of reliability, occur all over the United States and Canada, but they are primarily concentrated in the wilderness of Northern California, Washington State, Oregon, Alaska, and British Columbia. Mount Saint Helens, site of the famous Ape Canyon incident in 1924, was once a hot spot for Sasquatch encounters, along with Bluff Creek, California, and the Blue Mountains near Walla Walla, Washington. The Appalachian Mountains of eastern North America have also been home to Bigfoot sightings, particularly along Chestnut Ridge, which stretches from West Virginia up through Western Pennsylvania. Bigfoot hunters have also concentrated their efforts on a particular region in Wyoming, located somewhere between Cody and Yellowstone National Park. Even the Florida Everglades may hide a Bigfoot, or perhaps one of the creature's relatives.

According to the Bigfoot Field Researchers Organization (BFRO), which identifies itself as the only scientific research organization exploring the Bigfoot/Sasquatch mystery, there have been 5,162 sightings of Bigfoot/Sasquatch/Yeti-type creatures in the United States alone as of March 2018. Sightings have occurred in every state except Hawaii, with Washington (649 sightings) and California (437 sightings) leading the pack. There have been 293 sightings in Canada, with the majority (130) occurring in British Columbia. Sightings have also been reported in Malaysia (36), Australia (1), China (11), the Himalayan region (10), Indonesia (3), and Russia (5).

CONDITIONS FOR SIGHTINGS

Bigfoot sightings usually occur in remote areas with very low human populations and in places that have an annual rainfall of 20 inches (51 cm). It should also be noted that most Bigfoot sightings occur in areas that also are home to bears. Skeptics have long suspected that Bigfoot encounters are nothing more than misapprehended bear sightings. Even some Bigfoot experts believe that 70 percent to 80 percent of all alleged sightings are either hoaxes or mistaken identification of other animals.

Many sightings take place at night, alongside lonely stretches of road at the fringes of civilization. Numerous eyewitnesses have reported that Bigfoot's eyes reflected light like those of a cat, appearing to glow red or yellow or green. A pungent and unpleasant odor emanates from the furry creature, which is strongly recalled by almost everyone who encounters Bigfoot. Very rarely is more than one Sasquatch seen at a time, and usually for only as long as it takes for the creature to disappear back into the murky shadows of the forest.

The plaster of paris cast of an alleged Bigfoot print was produced by tractor operator Gerald Crew in 1958. He poses with the cast in the background here, providing scale for the size of the print.

TRACKS

Perhaps the most persuasive evidence of Bigfoot's presence is the gigantic footprints that inspired the creature's popular nickname. Often more than 14 inches (36 cm) long, the tracks, which resemble the impression of a bare human foot, are too large and wide to belong to a human being or even a gorilla (which only exist in captivity in North America). The prints also sink much deeper than any corresponding human footprints, seeming to confirm that they were left behind by something bigger and heavier than any ordinary human being. The prints are usually found in wet soil, soft earth, mud, or snow and have often been discovered not far from where Bigfoot sightings had previously occurred. The spacing of the tracks suggests that the creature has an enormous stride (more than 3 feet, or 91 cm) and that it can easily step over obstacles such as fences and boulders.

Careful analysis of the most credible and seemingly authentic tracks reveals an astonishing degree of detail, including impressions of realistic wrinkles and ridges—known as dermal ridges and akin to fingerprints—in the fleshy parts of the creature's feet. Many of these prints also feature a so-called midtarsal break, which is a distinctive pattern formed when an ape's foot bends before taking the next stride. Human feet do not do this. Furthermore, subtle differences between human and Sasquatch footprints make sense anatomically, when Bigfoot's superior size and weight are taken into account. Anyone faking these tracks would have to possess an extensive knowledge of human and ape anatomy, as well as a thorough understanding of the physics of bipedal locomotion.

Yet it should be noted that mistakes can be made when examining these kinds of "footprints." Bear prints can often be mistaken for those of a Bigfoot. In addition, tightly clumped tracks of an animal or animals can appear to be a single large footprint. Any smaller footprints or tracks made in snow can begin to appear much larger and differently shaped as the snow melts.

Although footprints are the most common type of impression left behind by Bigfoot, other kinds of tracks have occasionally been found as well. Hand and knuckle prints, possibly created when a Sasquatch stumbled and/or began to rise from a sitting position, reveal that Bigfoot's hands are also larger and wider than an adult human's hands. The palm is broad and flat, and the fingers are stubby. These creatures also seem to lack an opposable thumb, something confirmed by a number of eyewitness reports.

In 2000, an expert team from the BFRO left fruit in the middle of a muddy portion of the Skookum

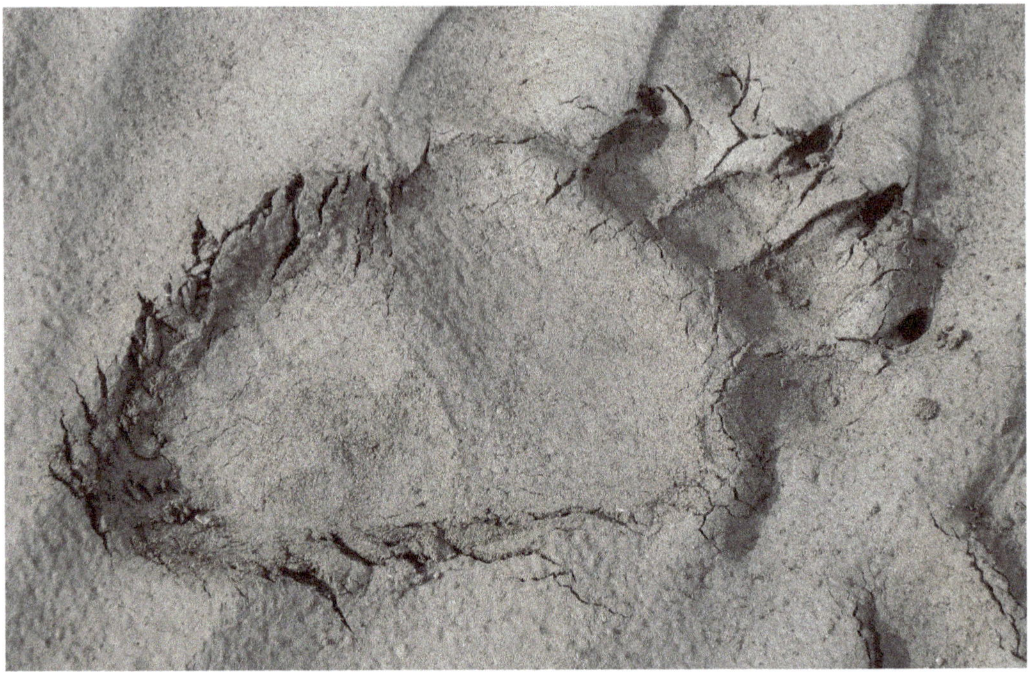

Bear footprints, like the one in this riverbed, can be mistaken for Bigfoot tracks. The condition of the ground is one thing to consider when analyzing any print since environmental factors can alter prints over time.

Meadows area of Gifford Pinchot National Park in Washington State. The fruit served as bait, and some kind of animal did indeed leave its impression in the mud. The BFRO team made casts of this impression and firmly believe it to be the forearm, hip, thigh, heel, ankle, and Achilles tendon of a Bigfoot. Some Bigfoot experts agreed, while others thought it more likely that the impression was made by an elk. Elk hoof and coyote paw prints appear in the cast, and both elk and bear hair were also detected. A retired biomedical researcher analyzed this hair and claimed it was from a single creature, which he believed to be a

Sasquatch. He admitted, however, that there was no way to test or prove this claim.

THE EYE-OPENING PATTERSON-GIMLIN FILM

Perhaps the most famous, controversial, and hotly debated piece of evidence for the existence of Bigfoot is 952 frames of color film footage shot by a man named Roger Patterson in Bluff Creek, California, in October 1967. The footage appears to show a full-grown Sasquatch striding confidently along a sunlit creek bed littered with fallen timber and other debris from the stream. At one point, the Bigfoot, which is covered with dark black fur, looks back at the filmmaker before walking farther away, at which point the camera ran out of film.

Bigfoot tracks had often been found in this region of Northern California, including some discovered earlier that summer. Patterson and his friend Bob Gimlin had been searching for Bigfoot on horseback when they supposedly stumbled onto the creature at Bluff Creek. Later, after losing track of the immense black figure in the woods, Patterson and Gimlin made casts of the creature's footprints, which were over 2 feet (61 cm) long.

The brief snippet of footage filmed by Patterson and Gimlin, which runs slightly less than two minutes, has been analyzed and argued about for more than five decades, and copies of the video can be viewed online.

Although it has frequently been dismissed as a hoax, this has never been proved, and many experts continue to vouch for its authenticity.

A persistent rumor exists that the "Bigfoot" in the film is actually an actor wearing a costume created by John Chambers, the famous Hollywood makeup artist who won an Academy Award for his work on the original *Planet of the Apes* movies (the first film in the series was released in 1968). However, Chambers denied any part in the incident. He did once create a large stone Bigfoot prop designed for use in a carnival, as well as a giant Iceman that was displayed in midwestern state fairs, but he claimed not to have known Patterson and Gimlin at

These still images break down the dramatic sequence in the famous Patterson-Gimlin film when the Bigfoot creature turns to look at the camera as it passes.

the time of their filming. He further claimed that he was a good makeup artist but not good enough to create something as convincing as the creature that appears in the Patterson-Gimlin film. Many people have also pointed out that the actors in the *Planet* films are merely wearing masks that cover the head, face, and neck and have prosthetic hands—not full-body suits.

FURTHER BRUSHES WITH BIGFOOT

During a 1996 fishing trip at Chopaka Lake in Washington State, Lori Pate and her family members twice sighted a large, apelike creature walking on two feet. The third sighting was captured on film, as the supposed Bigfoot runs across a hill and then walks into a group of trees. Later forensic tests and measurements concluded that this creature was about 5 feet tall (1.6 m), had a leg length of 2.5 feet (76 cm), was running at about 8.5 miles per hour (13.8 km/hr), and had a stride of 4.25 feet (1.3 m). This video was examined, dissected, and discussed in the 2003 documentary *Sasquatch: Legend Meets Science,* aired by the Discovery Channel. Pate's footage is also widely available online.

Northwestern Pennsylvania has not been particularly famous for Bigfoot sightings, yet in 2007 a man named Rick Jacobs photographed what he and the BFRO described as a juvenile Bigfoot. Hoping only to photograph deer, Jacobs sprinkled an aromatic deer attractant mix at the base of a tree. The bait worked, and Jacobs photographed both deer and bear cubs that wandered to the site to investi-

HOLLYWOOD BOUND

The John Chambers rumor is believed to have been started by the Hollywood director John Landis, best known for the movies *Animal House* (1978), *The Blues Brothers* (1980), *An American Werewolf in London* (1981), and the 1983 music video for Michael Jackson's song "Thriller." Landis and Chambers both worked on *Beneath the Planet of the Apes* in 1973. In that same year, Landis hired Chambers for a bit part in *Schlock*, Landis's first directing job, a comedy about a Bigfoot-like creature that terrorizes college students.

A student of Chambers, Rick Baker, created the ape-man costume and makeup for *Schlock*, and he would later create the Bigfoot costume and makeup for the movie *Harry and the Hendersons* (1987). He would also work on the 1976 *King Kong* remake, *Greystoke: The Legend of Tarzan, Lord of the Apes* (1984), *Werewolf* (1987), *Gorillas in the Mist* (1988), *Missing Link* (1988), *Wolf* (1994), the 2001 remake of *Planet of the Apes*, and *The Wolfman* (2010).

gate the smell. Yet so too did an unidentifiable creature that was about the size of an adolescent bear, with dark fur covering its entire body but with more apelike anatomy. It appears to press its face to the ground to smell the mixture. This posture echoes more closely the way an ape would bend to smell the earth than the way a bear would. Yet officials from the Pennsylvania Game Commission confidently declared that this mysterious apelike creature was merely a young, skinny bear with mange.

Footage of a Bigfoot creature has even been captured on a dashboard camera like the one here. The Georgia state police cruiser's controversial 2009 footage can be found online.

In August 2017, another incident was reported in another part of the United States. In western North Carolina, a Sasquatch enthusiast group known as Bigfoot 911, which boasts nearly ten thousand members, placed glow sticks in multiple locations in McDowell County in hopes of luring Bigfoot out of the woods. According to John E. Bruner, who runs the group's Facebook page, they were successful. As Bruner explains, "I turned my headlamp on and I saw a large bi-pedal animal covered in hair. It took one step into the woods, (then) I took off running toward where it went into the woods." Bruner and some of the others in the group who were present tried to follow the creature, but it was too fast. Bruner concludes, "It turned and took five steps and was at the bottom of the hill, probably 30 yards. I could see the gluteus maximus flexing with each step."

The intriguing amount of detail in these and other encounters is one of the driving factors in the search for Sasquatch—and for any other cryptids out there.

CHAPTER FOUR

OTHER CRYPTIDS AND THE NATURE OF HOAXES

There are many other creatures across the world that may or may not be related to Bigfoot. In any case, it's worth remembering that early humans are known to have coexisted with *Gigantopithecus*, the Neanderthals, and many other prehistoric humanlike creatures. What's more, many of these humanlike beings survived for millions of years before (supposedly) becoming extinct. Given that all of recorded history is far less than fifty thousand years, just a tiny sliver of time in the ongoing evolution of humanity, it should not be too surprising to find out that humanity is not really as unique as people might suspect.

THE YETI OF THE HIMALAYAS

Beyond a doubt, Bigfoot's most famous relative is the Yeti, also known as the Abominable Snowman. Said to live in the snowy peaks of the Himalayan mountains, the Yeti is occasionally glimpsed by explorers and mountain climbers attempting to scale Mount Everest or one of the other surrounding peaks. Its bare footprints have also been discovered from time to time, sunken deep into the stark white snow. Like Bigfoot, the Yeti is well known

Though the Himalayas are primarily known for their high, snowy peaks, there are also tropical and subtropical forests at the base of the mountains, making the region home to an incredibly diverse array of species.

to its region's indigenous population, in this case the people of Tibet and Nepal. The Yeti has deep roots in Tibetan and Nepalese religion and folklore. In fact, the name "Yeti" comes from the Sherpa term *yet-teh*, which can be loosely translated as "small, manlike animal."

The mountain-dwelling monster did not become world famous, however, until 1921, when members of a British expedition to Mount Everest spotted dimly seen figures moving high on the mountain slopes. At that high-elevation spot, the explorers later found a set of large, unexplained footprints. A Calcutta newspaper reported the incident, referring to the unknown creature as the Abominable Snowman. This was nothing more than a mistranslation of another Sherpa phrase, which actually meant something like "man-sized snow creature." The more colorful name quickly caught on with the public, however, and the story of the Abominable Snowman soon spread across the planet.

Since then, several expeditions have set out in search of the Yeti, while others have attempted (unsuccessfully) to debunk the legend. One popular theory holds that the Snowman does not actually live in the mountains themselves but in the secluded jungle valleys between the peaks, only occasionally crossing the frozen slopes to get from one valley to another.

THE SKUNK APE OF THE EVERGLADES

Closer to home, the Skunk Ape may or may not be a separate and distinct species of Bigfoot found throughout the South, including North Carolina and Arkansas. The majority of sightings, however, have occurred in the Florida Keys and Everglades. Like the Sasquatch of the Pacific Northwest, the Skunk Ape is a smelly, apelike creature whose actual existence remains not only unproved but also unacknowledged by modern science. The Skunk Ape, whose strong and unpleasant odor has offended the nostrils of just about every witness who ever encountered the semimythical creature, first gained widespread notoriety during the

1970s. Some theories state that its characteristic noxious odor is a defense mechanism. In order to keep people away, the Skunk Ape rolls in dead carcasses to pick up a putrid smell.

In December 2000, two intriguing color photos were mailed to the Sheriff's Department in Sarasota, Florida. They were accompanied by a letter from a woman who claimed she took these photos from her backyard after an apelike creature that she believed to be an orangutan had taken apples from a bushel basket on her porch. The eye-catching pictures capture two views of a shaggy, gray-haired creature with a silvery beard. Two red eyes reflect the glare of the flashbulbs.

Robert Robinson, a former military-police officer and self-proclaimed "Legend Tripper," has gone on Skunk Ape expeditions with the BFRO. He has collected evidence of the Skunk Ape, including footprints. Robinson believes he caught sight of the creature twice, once with a thermal camera, or a camera that forms an image using infrared radiation. The hotter an object, the more radiation it emits, so thermal cameras capture heat signatures of the surrounding area and allow the person recording to discern the shapes of objects and organisms nearby. Firefighters use thermal cameras to help them find people or animals, and paranormal investigators of all kinds use them in their search for ghosts and other cryptids as well. In Robinson's case, he caught a glimpse of a bipedal creature in the distance after a fellow investigator alerted him to movement. The creature ran away, so they didn't get a good look at it, but after reexamining the situation later, they concluded the

Loren Coleman poses with the "Crookston Bigfoot," which many regard as the best-looking Bigfoot replica in existence. It can be viewed at the International Cryptozoology Museum in Portland, Maine.

creature must have been around 8 feet (2.4 m) tall.

Is the Skunk Ape simply a southern variety of Bigfoot, or a different kind of anthropoid altogether? Some reports, like Robinson's, describe a tall, bipedal primate much like a traditional Sasquatch, whom, it should be recalled, is also usually described as being extremely foul smelling. Other sightings, however, seem to involve a much smaller and more apelike creature, comparable to a chimpanzee or small orangutan. Some noted cryptozoologists, such as Loren Coleman, author of numerous books on the subject, believe that there may actually be two separate types of unknown primates lurking behind the lush foliage of the Florida Everglades.

OTHER BIPEDAL CRYPTIDS

The Yeti and the Skunk Ape are only two of the most notable anthropoids believed to be hiding in the world's

BIGFOOT HOAXES

Even some cryptozoologists who are inclined to believe in at least the possible existence of Bigfoot claim that the vast majority of sightings are either misidentification of other animals, like bears, or are outright hoaxes. Not only is the deliberate filmed staging of a Bigfoot sighting, the fabrication of footprints, or the phony discovery of fake Bigfoot hair or even an entire Bigfoot carcass a violation of the truth, it also muddies the scientific picture, making it that much harder to arrive at firm conclusions regarding the existence of Sasquatch.

The credibility of Bigfoot studies and the science behind it are particularly undermined when hoaxes are devised by prominent members of the Bigfoot research community. One such case occurred in 2005, when Tom Biscardi, the CEO of Searching for Bigfoot, Inc., a for-profit organization that claims to investigate eyewitness accounts of Bigfoot encounters, made several appearances on a paranormal-themed, nationally syndicated radio show. During one radio interview, he first claimed that his group was tracking a Bigfoot in California and that a capture was imminent. In a later appearance, he claimed to have access to a captured Bigfoot and was arranging for a public viewing of it via pay-per-view television. Finally, in yet another radio interview, he claimed that he had been duped and that there was no captured

(continued on the next page)

(continued from the previous page)

Bigfoot. The community of Bigfoot enthusiasts generally believe that Biscardi, far from being duped, was the one fabricating the entire story.

An even more outlandish hoax was perpetrated three years later and captured the world's attention thanks to YouTube. An amateur video shot by Rick Dyer and Matthew Whitton purporting to show a deceased Bigfoot found in northern Georgia went viral soon after it was posted. Ironically, Biscardi was brought in to provide an "independent" investigation. He also paid Dyer and Whitton $50,000. Upon closer inspection of the carcass, however, it was discovered that the hair was fake, the head was hollow, and the feet were made of plastic. Dyer and Whitton were forced to admit their perpetration of a hoax. Biscardi's exact role in the events remains unclear, as does what he knew and when he knew it.

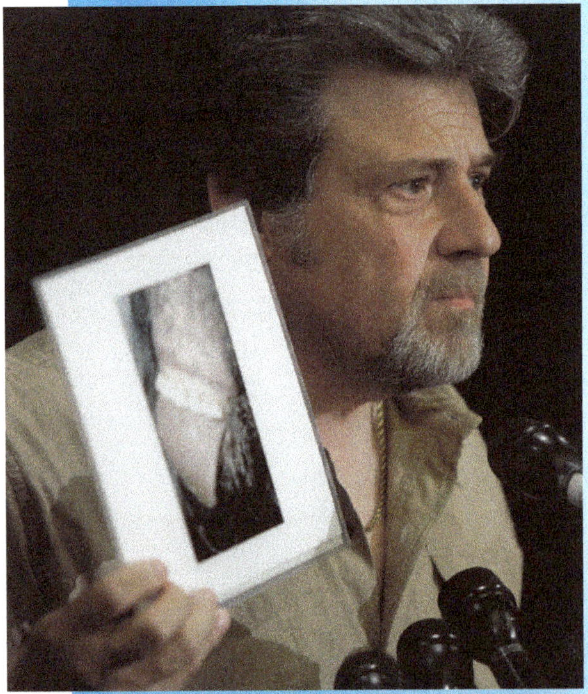

At a 2008 news conference, Bigfoot hunter Tom Biscardi presents a photo of what he claims to be the mouth and teeth of a deceased Bigfoot creature. The discovery was later proved to be a hoax.

diverse wilderness regions. Indonesia, for one, boasts myths of the Ebu Gogo, a group of hairy, human-esque creatures. They run quickly, are about 5 feet (1.5 meters) tall, and frequently kidnap children in folktales, though the children always outwit the cryptids and get away. Some suspect the Ebu Gogo are connected to *Homo floresiensis*, an extinct hominin that may have lived as recently as thirteen thousand years ago. The specimens

DEBUNK IT!

British paleontologist and science writer Darren Naish has devoted some of his work to discussing the search for cryptids, including a 2016 book entitled *Hunting Monsters*. His study includes the search for Bigfoot, and in a June 2016 article for *Scientific American* called "If Bigfoot Were Real," Naish offers the following reasons why he's skeptical of Bigfoot's existence:

- **Recordings of Bigfoot "howls" would be "biologically consistent" across North America, meaning they should all sound very similar across the Bigfoot species.**
- **Footprints or other tracks would be easily found by professional trackers.**
- **Bigfoot prints would not seem so clean or purposeful but would be more natural. For**

(continued on the next page)

(continued from the previous page)

example, a person's boot prints in snow tend to look different from print to print, since the foot descends into the snow and the level of snow varies over the ground. Similarly, Bigfoot's footprints in the mud or soft earth would vary.

- **Bigfoot DNA would be all over the places where encounters were reported. All instances of DNA findings to date have been debunked and linked to other mammals, so if Bigfoot is so prevalent, how has its DNA not been collected and identified by now?**

Naish adds that most footage and other evidence is copyrighted by the discoverers, which is suspicious if one is honestly trying to share the truth about such a creature. His conclusion is that Bigfoot sightings are the result of "a sociocultural phenomenon: that people are seeing all manner of different things, combining [them] with ideas, memes and preconceptions they hold in their minds, and interpreting them as encounters with a monstrous, human-like biped."

discovered on the Indonesian island of Flores in 2004 included one complete skull and partial skeletons of several of the hominins, and the species has been nicknamed the "Flores Man."

On Mainland China, the mysterious Yeren, a shaggy, red-haired wild man, has been the subject of extensive research and speculation. Unfortunately, when it comes to acquiring definitive proof of the Yeren's existence,

Chinese cryptozoologists have not had any better luck than their North American counterparts, so the true nature of the Yeren remains unknown. Yet in 2010, reports surfaced that a team of Chinese researchers at the Shennongjia Nature Reserve were examining unidentified hair believed to be from a Yeren, often referred to in North America as Hubei Bigfoot.

Meanwhile, Russian scholars speak of the Almas of Mongolia, who may or may not be the last surviving remnants of Neanderthals. And Down Under, on the continent of Australia, there are occasional sightings of a Yowie, which sounds an awful lot like a Sasquatch—except that it only has four toes on each foot. And cryptozoologists are still searching the jungles of Sumatra for the Orang Pendek, a 5-foot-tall (1.5 m), bipedal primate. One thing that makes the Orang Pendek unique is that even skeptics who scoff at Bigfoot and the Yeti concede that the Orang Pendek probably exists.

CHAPTER FIVE

BIGFOOT ON THE BRAIN

Dizzying reports and failed scientific expeditions aside, Bigfoot remains in the collective consciousness. No matter the veracity, or truthfulness, of Bigfoot's existence, the mysterious anthropoid has been the subject of documentaries and is a staple of the "weird news" sections of newspapers and magazines. Sasquatch has also been, and continues to be, included in all manner of fiction, from movies and television to comics and video games.

ON SCREENS BIG AND SMALL

Since the 1970s, more than thirty-five major films have been released that feature a Bigfoot story or include a Bigfoot-like creature as a character or plot point. These range from action dramas and horror movies to comedies and spoofs. One famous docudrama, or documentary featuring reenacted real-life events, was the 1972 feature, *The Legend of Boggy Creek*. The film was about the "Fouke Monster," a Bigfoot creature encountered around Fouke, Arkansas, since the 1950s.

In television, one of the best-known shows to feature Bigfoot is the family comedy-drama *Harry and the Hen-*

dersons, which was spawned by a 1987 film of the same name. In the show, a family returning from a camping trip hits and injures a Sasquatch with their car. They take it home and nurse it back to health. Once recovered, the good-natured but wild Bigfoot wreaks havoc in the Henderson's house and neighborhood. Eventually, as law enforcement officials and hunters close in, the family decides to release "Harry" back to the wild.

Most North Americans first "encountered" Bigfoot through television quasi-documentary, cryptozoological investigative programs like *In Search of...*, hosted by Leonard Nimoy (*Star Trek*'s Mr. Spock). Bigfoot became a sensation among young people when the creature, enhanced by bionic technology, had a recurring role on the popular 1970s action show *The Six Million Dollar Man* and its spin-off, *The Bionic Woman.* Today, Bigfoot continues to appear regularly on popular investigative documentaries airing on the History Channel, Discovery, Animal Planet, and A&E, among other cable networks. Even actor Rob Lowe has been involved in the Bigfoot television

The cast of Animal Planet's *Finding Bigfoot* speaks at a discussion panel in 2012. Matt Moneymaker (*far right*) also founded the BFRO.

scene, premiering his show *The Lowe Files* in 2017. The show features Lowe and his two sons as they investigate mysteries and paranormal events around the United States, including an episode in which they believe they've encountered a Bigfoot creature.

YOUTUBE, VIDEO GAMES, AND MERCHANDISE

Bigfoot is not only a star of the silver screen and an enduring television personality. The creature has also become a cyber-celebrity, daily appearing on personal computer screens worldwide. When Bigfoot's name is typed into YouTube's search engine, more than two million results appear, and new videos are added all the time. These run the gamut from earnest amateur sightings and famous footage like the Patterson-Gimlin film to clever hoaxes, over-the-top comedic spoofs, mockumentaries, and film trailers.

Bigfoot has also become a popular character in video and computer games. In most of these games, Bigfoot has only a cameo role or can be a playable character (as in *The Simpsons, Tony Hawk's Underground 2*, and the *Darkstalkers* series). Yet in some, like *Sam and Max Hit the Road,* the game centers on the search for and attempted recapture of a Bigfoot escaped from a carnival. In 2010, Rockstar Games released downloadable content, or DLC, for its hit game *Red Dead Redemption* that included a mission to hunt a Sasquatch cryptid.

In the more analog 1970s and 1980s, Bigfoot inspired board games, pinball machines, action figures, store-bought Halloween costumes, and lunch boxes. There were even Bigfoot snowshoes, guaranteed to leave behind massive footprints in the snow. While these products are no longer manufactured, they remain hot commodities among collectors, who engage in heated and high-priced bidding wars for them on auction websites like eBay.

This 1977 action figure is of the Bionic Bigfoot, which was introduced in one of the best-known story lines of *The Six Million Dollar Man*, a two-part episode entitled "The Secret of Bigfoot."

GRAPHIC NOVELS AND COMICS

The ordinarily highly elusive Sasquatch is frequently spotted among the pages of comic books, graphic novels, graphic nonfiction, and traditional novels. The creature also routinely makes headlines in sensationalistic supermarket tabloids such as the *National Enquirer.*

Bigfoot is also the star of his own comic book series called *Proof.* In it, Bigfoot actually works as a sort of cryptozoologist and, in conjunction with a secret government agency, searches for other mysterious creatures, including the Chupacabra, jackalopes, dinosaurs, and fairies, among others.

In the four-comic-book series *Savage,* Bigfoot is revealed to be a man who transforms into a beast. This transformative ability can be passed from one man to another, and the resulting Bigfoot creature is charged with protecting humanity from danger—in this case a terrorizing pack of werewolves.

A more sinister man-Bigfoot transformation is achieved by the Marvel Comics character Dr. Walter Langkowski. Due to gamma radiation experiments gone bad, he has the ability to transform into an orange-furred, astoundingly powerful creature who calls himself Sasquatch. He is almost immune to cold, has sharp claws and teeth, and can leap vast distances. He frequently both battles against and joins forces with various X-Men, the Hulk, and other Marvel superheroes.

Numerous young adult novels feature Bigfoot, including Eric S. Brown's *Bigfoot War,* in which a young man seeks to avenge the murder of his family by a Sasquatch, and Dallas Tanner's *Track of the Bigfoot,* in which a childhood encounter with Bigfoot leads to the protagonist's later scientific search for the creature. In addition, hundreds of nonfiction titles about Bigfoot and the search for the creature are available. Some of the more intriguing include *Enoch: A Bigfoot Story,* by Autumn Williams; *Impossible Visits: The Inside Story of Interactions with Sasquatch at Habituation Sites,* by Christopher Noel; *Valley of the Skookum: Four Years of Encounters with Bigfoot,* by Sali Sheppard-Wolford; *Sasquatch: Legend Meets Science,* by Jeff Meldrum; *Bigfoot!: The True Story of Apes in America,* by Loren Coleman; and *Bigfoot Observer's Field Manual: A Practical and Easy-to-Follow Step-by-Step Guide to Your Very Own Face-to-Face Encounter with a Legend,* by Robert W. Morgan.

BIGFOOT ON THE MARKETING SCENE

Over the years, Bigfoot has become an influential celebrity pitchman, lending his name and image to a wide range of products, including campers, monster trucks, beer, wine, gas stations, skateboards, skis, pizzas, an internet search engine, computer hard drives, and even beef jerky. In fact, the company behind the Jack Link's brand of beef jerky has run a series of commercials in which various outdoorsmen play practical jokes on Bigfoot, sending the creature into a murderous rage.

Numerous tourist attractions, primarily in the Pacific Northwest, use the Bigfoot/Sasquatch name and image to promote restaurants, motels, gift shops, and amusement parks. Sasquatch has even been used as a sports mascot. "Quatchi," a young Canadian sasquatch, was

Quatchi, seen here skating at the GE Ice Plaza in Vancouver, Canada, in November 2009, was one of a group of Olympic Games mascots based on popular cryptids.

a mascot for the 2010 Vancouver Winter Olympics, and "Squatch" is the Bigfoot mascot for the professional Seattle SuperSonics basketball team. There is even a Big Foot High School in Walworth, Wisconsin.

BELIEVE IT OR NOT

In the end, it hardly matters whether Bigfoot, Sasquatch, the Yeti, the Skunk Ape, and other mysterious and elusive ape-men continue to lurk in the world's remaining dense forests, swamps, and mountain valleys or merely

SASQUATCH FESTIVALS

The town of Willow Creek, California, self-proclaimed capital of "Bigfoot Country" and near the spot where the first casts of a Sasquatch footprint were made in 1958, hosts an annual Bigfoot Days festival over the Labor Day weekend. Kicking off with a parade led by Bigfoot himself, the festival also includes a car show, live bands, food and craft booths, and an ice-cream social at the Willow Creek–China Flat Museum, whose

This Bigfoot exhibit is periodically updated as new donations related to Bigfoot come in. The large wooden statue outside provides a permanent photo opportunity for enthusiasts and tourists alike.

(continued on the next page)

(continued from the previous page)

most prominent feature is a Bigfoot exhibition that includes Bigfoot pictures and footprint casts, maps, other Bigfoot-related papers and documents, and a research center.

Sasquatch has even become associated with several major festivals. The annual Sasquatch! Music Festival is held over Memorial Day weekend at an outdoor amphitheater in George, Washington. There are four stages: the Bigfoot Stage, the Yeti Stage, the Sasquatch! Main Stage, and the Rumpus Room. In 2018, the festival included Wolf Parade, Nao, Whitney, the Suffers, Taco, Modest Mouse, Spoon, Explosions in the Sky, Grizzly Bear, Algiers, Curtis Harding, Polyrhythmics, Wilderado, the National, Neko Case, What So Not, Slowdive, Phoebe Bridgers, Typhoon, (Sandy) Alex G, Tyler, the Creator, and many others.

in people's fevered imaginations. Whether they are surviving remnants of a primeval past, wild creatures roaming free, or elaborate hoaxes, what does matter is the possibility that such a creature exists and humanity's desire to believe it is true. Modern humans—logical, civilized, and technologically advanced—have a powerful need to believe there are still mysteries to be solved, pristine wildernesses to discover, and previously unknown and unimagined creatures to encounter.

GLOSSARY

anthropoid A creature resembling a human; the term is usually applied to the higher apes, such as the chimpanzee, gorilla, orangutan, and gibbon.

Bigfoot A popular nickname for a mysterious apelike creature believed to live deep in the forests of North America. The term, inspired by the large tracks discovered in Humboldt County, California, was first used by the *Humboldt Times*, in 1958.

bionic Having normal human abilities enhanced by electrical or electromechanical devices or artificial body parts.

bipedal Describes any animal that goes about on two feet.

cryptid Any mysterious or legendary creature whose existence is not yet accepted or proved by modern science.

cryptozoology The study of mystery animals whose existence has been reported but not yet scientifically proved.

dashboard camera A camera designed to mount on the inner side of a car windshield and continuously record while the car is in motion. Also known as a dash cam.

docudrama A documentary that features dramatic reenactments of true events.

hoax A falsehood intended to deceive others into believing something is true, particularly something outrageous or paranormal.

hominid Members of the biological family *Hominidae*, including all species of two-legged primates, extinct and living.

hominoid Members of the larger superfamily *Hominoi-*

dae, including humans, great apes, and gibbons. Not to be confused with hominid.

noxious Physically harmful or posing a harmful influence on one's behavior or mental state.

opposable thumb A digit that can be placed opposite the fingers of the same hand, allowing the hand to grasp and handle things.

oral tradition The passing down of stories, beliefs, customs, and other information by word of mouth within a cultural group.

prehistory A time that precedes the existence of written records.

primate A specific order of mammals with especially flexible hands and feet, each with five digits. Includes humans, apes, monkeys, and lemurs.

sagittal crest A bony ridge running lengthwise across the top of a skull, between the right and left halves of the skull. Exhibited by male gorillas and orangutans and some female gorillas.

Sasquatch Another name for Bigfoot, loosely derived from "Sesquac" and other similar-sounding Canadian Indian terms. Coined in the 1920s by a Canadian journalist, J. W. Burns, to label the large, hairy giants described in the myths and folklore of First Nation Canadian tribes. Now used more or less interchangeably with "Bigfoot."

species A biological classification that describes a group of organisms that can potentially reproduce with each other.

veracity Accuracy or conformity to truth.

British Columbia Scientific Cryptozoology Club (BCSCC)
8805 Hudson Street, Suite 2305
Vancouver, BC, Canada V6P 4M9
Website: http://bcscc.ca/blog
Founded by journalists and scientists, the BCSCC is Canada's leading cryptozoology organization.

International Cryptozoology Museum
661 Congress Street
Portland, ME 04104
(207) 518-9496
Website: http://www.cryptozoologymuseum.com
Facebook: @cryptozoologymuseum
Billed as the world's only fully public cryptozoology museum, the exhibits include an 8-foot-tall (2.4 m), 400-pound (181 kg) Bigfoot, a mermaid, a thunderbird, and other "mysteries of the world."

OregonBigfoot.com
PO Box 24332
Eugene, OR 97402
Website: http://www.oregonbigfoot.com
Oregon Bigfoot is not a research organization, but rather a community of incidental Bigfoot witnesses, long-term witnesses, independent investigators, and those with a keen interest in this subject. Its members hail from all parts of the United States and across the world and have created one of the largest databases of Bigfoot sightings and other Bigfoot-related information.

Ripley's Believe It or Not! Times Square
234 West Forty-Second Street
New York, NY 10036
(212) 398-3133
Website: http://www.ripleysnewyork.com
Twitter and Instagram: @RipleysNY
For over forty years, Robert Ripley traveled the world collecting the unbelievable, the inexplicable, and the one-of-a-kind. His vast collections are now on display, including hundreds of weird and unusual artifacts.

Sasquatch Information Society
PO Box 48333
Seattle, WA 98148
Website: http://www.bigfootinfo.org
A database containing Bigfoot news, articles, links, polls, events, sightings, interviews, and research.

Sasquatch Investigations of the Rockies, Inc.
PO Box 4566
Parker, CO 80134
Website: http://www.sasquatchinvestigations.org
Sasquatch Investigations of the Rockies is a Bigfoot research group based in Parker, Colorado. The purpose of the organization is to spend as much time as possible in the target areas of the Rocky Mountains documenting the legendary Bigfoot/Sasquatch. The group's most compelling data to date is available on its website.

Searching for Bigfoot, Inc.
1134 Crane Street, Suite 216
Menlo Park, CA 94025
(650) 566-4001
Website: http://www.searchingforbigfoot.com
Facebook: @searchingforbigfootinc
An organization that purports to investigate eyewitness accounts of Bigfoot sightings.

North American Wood Ape Conservancy
PO Box 2162
Belton, TX 76513
Website: http://www.woodape.org
Facebook: @noamwoodape
The North American Wood Ape Conservancy is a non-profit scientific-research organization composed of volunteer investigators, scientists, and naturalists who pursue education and research activities pertaining to the centuries-old "wildman" or "hairy man" phenomenon in North America.

FOR FURTHER READING

Bougie, Matt. *Bigfoot, the Loch Ness Monster, and Unexplained Creatures* (Paranormal Investigations). New York, NY: Cavendish Square Publishing, 2018.

Chambers, Catherine. *Bigfoot*. Chicago, IL: Heinemann Raintree, 2016.

Freeburg, Jessica. *Monsters of the Midwest: True Tales of Bigfoot, Werewolves & Other Legendary Creatures*. Cambridge, MN: Adventure Publications, 2016.

Holm, Deanna. *An Adventure in Tropical & Temperate Rainforests*. Poulsbo, WA: Kitsap Publishing, 2017.

Loh-Hagan, Virginia. *Bigfoot: Magic, Myth, and Mystery*. Ann Arbor, MI: Cherry Lake Publishing, 2017.

Niver, Heather Moore. *Investigating Bigfoot, the Loch Ness Monster, and Other Cryptids* (Understanding the Paranormal). New York, NY: Britannica Educational Publishing, 2017.

Redfern, Nicholas. *The Bigfoot Book: The Encyclopedia of Sasquatch, Yeti, and Cryptid Primates*. Detroit, MI: Visible Ink Press, 2016.

Rich, Mari. *Rescuing Primates: Gorillas, Chimps, and Monkeys*. Broomall, PA: Mason Crest, 2018.

Ridley, Kimberly. *Extreme Survivors: Animals That Time Forgot*. Thomaston, ME: Tilbury House Publishers, 2017.

Shepherd, Courtney A. *A Field Guide to the Cryptids of North America*. Minneapolis, MN: Howecycle Press, 2017.

Strand, Jennifer. *Jane Goodall*. Minneapolis, MN: Abdo Zoom, 2017.

BIBLIOGRAPHY

Bennett, Abbie. "Bigfoot in the Carolinas? Chupacabra? 'People See What They Want to See.'" *Raleigh (NC) News & Observer*, August 16, 2017. http://www.newsobserver.com/news/weird/article167562457.html.

Bigfoot Field Researchers Organization. "United States Sighting Reports." Retrieved February 28, 2018. http://www.bfro.net/GDB.

Bigley, Michele. *Backroads & Byways of Northern California: Day Trips and Weekend Excursions.* Woodstock, VT: Countryman Press, 2012.

Farlow, Susan. "You May Not Believe in Bigfoot or the Loch Ness Monster—but This Museum May Persuade You Otherwise." *Los Angeles Times*, January 23, 2017. http://www.latimes.com/travel/la-tr-cryptozoological-museum-20170122-story.html.

Finding Bigfoot. "Top 10 Bigfoot Sightings of the Last 5 Years." Animal Planet, 2012. http://www.animalplanet.com/tv-shows/finding-bigfoot/lists/10-bigfoot-sightings-last-5-years.

Hall, Travis. "Bigfoot Sighting Reported in Western North Carolina." *Blue Ridge Outdoors*, August 8, 2017. http://www.blueridgeoutdoors.com/go-outside/bigfoot-sighting-reported-western-north-carolina.

Huffaker, Christopher. "Allegheny County Leads the State in Reports of UFOs and Bigfoot." *Pittsburgh Post-Gazette*, July 31, 2017. http://www.post-gazette.com/local/region/2017/07/31/bigfoot-ufo-paranormal-sightings-kecksburg-allegheny-county-cryptids-thunderbirds-pittsburgh/stories/201707310058.

Ketchum, Melba S. "Novel North American Hominins, Next Generation Sequencing of Three Whole Genomes and

Associated Studies." Sasquatch Genome Project, 2012. http://www.sasquatchgenomeproject.org/linked/novel-north-american-hominins-final-pdf-download.pdf.

Kowalick, Claire. "Man Claims to Have Found Bigfoot Skull." *Wichita (TX) Times Record News*, June 2, 2016. http://archive.timesrecordnews.com/news/local/man-claims-to-have-found-bigfoot-skull-344d87ee-9377-04e6-e053-0100007f306a-381665331.html.

Mayell, Hillary. "Hobbit-Like Human Ancestor Found in Asia." *National Geographic News*, October 27, 2004. https://news.nationalgeographic.com/news/2004/10/1027_041027_homo_floresiensis.html.

Moraski, Lauren. "Did Rob Lowe Really See Bigfoot? Actor Sets the Record Straight."Huffington Post, August 1, 2017. https://www.huffingtonpost.com/entry/rob-lowe-the-lowe-files-bigfoot_us_596e1974e4b010d77673e022.

Naish, Darren. "If Bigfoot Were Real." *Scientific American*, June 27, 2016. https://blogs.scientificamerican.com/tetrapod-zoology/if-bigfoot-were-real.

Runnells, Charles. "Hunting for Ghosts, UFOs and the Skunk Ape at Fort Myers Paranormal Conference." *Fort Myers (FL) News-Press*, February 21, 2018. https://www.news-press.com/story/entertainment/2018/02/21/hunting-ghosts-ufos-and-skunk-ape-fort-myers-paranormal-conference/350914002.

Smith, Zane. *Six Rivers National Forest (N.F.), Chimney Rock/Gasquete-Orleans Road: Environmental Impact Statement*. Del Norte County, CA: US Department of Agriculture Forest Service, Pacific Southwest Region, 1982.

INDEX

ABOUT THE AUTHORS

Jenna Vale is a New Jersey native who has followed paranormal stories all her life. She has visited multiple sites of paranormal phenomena, from the dusty roads of *Weird NJ* fame to the haunted vaults of Edinburgh, Scotland.

Greg Cox grew up in Bigfoot country—the Pacific Northwest. He is the author of numerous books relating to science fiction, fantasy, superheroes, and unexplained mysteries.

PHOTO CREDITS

Cover ThePalmer/E+/Getty Images; pp. 1, 7, 16, 24, 34, 44 (background) sakkmesterke/Shutterstock.com; p. 3 iprostocks /Shutterstock.com; pp. 4–5 (background) Mordolff/E+/Getty Images; p. 5 Russ Bishop/Alamy Stock Photo; p. 8 Big_Ryan/DigitalVision Vectors/Getty Images; p. 9 Spencer Sutton/Science Source; p. 14 Des Bartlett/Science Source/Getty Images; pp. 15, 17, 40 © AP Images; p. 21 Alinari Archives/Getty Images; p. 23 Budimir Jevtic/Shutterstock .com; pp. 26, 51 Gary Crabbe/Enlightened Images/Alamy Stock Photo; p. 28 Bildagentur Zoonar GmbH/Shutterstock.com; p. 30 John Zada/Alamy Stock Photo; p. 33 Titikul_B/Shutterstock.com; p. 35 Westend61/Getty Images; p. 38 Portland Press Herald/Getty Images; p. 45 Frederick M. Brown/Getty Images; p. 47 www.benstoybarn.com/ Alamy Stock Photo; p. 50 Jeff Vinnick/Getty Images; cover, back cover, and interior pages (caution pattern) Geschaft/Shutterstock.com.

Design: Michael Moy; Editor: Megan Kellerman; Photo Researcher: Karen Huang